As Earth Begins to End

For Rusty —
So very well met in Austin —
I've been waiting a long time for
it, and it's been lovely —
Until next time —
Patricia G
3/10/06
(xxx to Ken too) —

As Earth Begins to End

NEW POEMS

Patricia Goedicke

COPPER CANYON PRESS

Grateful acknowledgment is made to Laura Popenoe
for the use of *East of the Sun* on the cover.

The publication of this book was supported by grants from the Lannan
Foundation, the National Endowment for the Arts, and the Washington
State Arts Commission. Additional support was received from Elliott Bay
Book Company, Cynthia Hartwig, and the many members who joined the
Friends of Copper Canyon Press campaign. Copper Canyon Press is in
residence with Centrum at Fort Worden State Park.

LIBRARY OF CONGRESS CATALOGING-IN-PUBLICATION DATA
Goedicke, Patricia.—
As earth begins to end: new poems / Patricia Goedicke.
p. cm.
ISBN 1-55659-134-9 (alk. paper)
I. Title.
PS3557.O32 A9 2000
811'.54 — DC2I   99-050526

3 5 7 9 8 6 4 2
FIRST PRINTING

COPPER CANYON PRESS
Post Office Box 271
Port Townsend, Washington 98368
www.coppercanyonpress.org

For Leonard

for we who are one body

Contents

As Earth Begins to End

I too but signify at the utmost a little washéd-up drift,
A few sands and dead leaves to gather,
Gather, and merge myself as part of the sands and drift.

— WALT WHITMAN
"As I Ebb'd with the Ocean of Life"

Matter: A witticism. At sub-atomic level,
that which has a tendency to exist.

— JEANETTE WINTERSON
Gut Symmetries

There's nothing that's not Nature.

— SAM HAMILL
"To Eron on Her Thirty-second Birthday"

Nagiko, I am waiting for you.
Meet me at the library?
Any library:
Every library.
Yours, Jerome

— FROM PETER GREENAWAY'S FILM
The Pillow Book

The Dreams We Wake From

are dams bursting, oceans suddenly swallowed
               by seas of blowing sand.
With lizard and jackrabbit skeletons, with cracked satellite dishes revolving
         like blisters on the glazed shell of the planet
   now all our newsreels are nightmares:
        in the latest, a charred hole melts
              on a giant screen, brown celluloid
       smokes, eats up the heroine's face, the
purple prairies, even Rockefeller Center, even the UN Building.
     As the cigarette circle smolders, in its thick sludge I slide
        right down into it;

Mother, your mouth is mine
        in every photograph album, your lips
          which are my lips, open onto an abyss
   like the spreading rim of a sinkhole, California
       hotels fall into themselves, executive suites,
      bathtubs, picture windows plane into swimming pools—

Here, let me take our minds
       off this, let me make up a story.
  But I can't finish it; this morning I woke up
        still hearing the slow, plot-driven
B-movie writer I'd been in my dream shouting
      as everything fell to pieces,

with no hint of any logical
      or even narrative structure to hold it,
    each scene dissolved, shattered into bricks, helicopters,

dead body parts and grenades flying straight at us
as they do in Beirut, Belfast, even in Brooklyn.
As Volkswagens blow up like babies, nowadays the old
carefully put together script leaves us

so hungry we gobble up, consume, *appropriate*
everything in sight and then blame ourselves,
blame "human nature," but who knows
what flexes and valences, what sparks
of strange protoplasm may be starting to hold hands
right now,
speak to each other in new food chains fused
to boiling bacteria shot
from stars we have yet to see?

No wonder she keeps playing pat-a-cake with us, from burned-out
projection booths sending us smashed kindergarten treatments
we'd never invent ourselves:
in such impossibly violent
jittering fantasies, what's really going on
was never clear anyway, but ignorant
as infants fresh from the petri dish, we know

Mother, your mouth is ours
always; even as it expands
the pink nipple of the universe drifts us
endlessly outward,
in millions of shattered pieces, specks of light flickering on and off
everywhere on its broad dreaming breast.....

What Holds Us Together

is almost nothing, a little
surface tension at the edges.

Inside ourselves, but how?

Two blood bottles,
weak capillaries in pajamas

rowing across the night.

Into whose arms, the
self says,

will I permit it, at last
let myself go, trust others

to receive me when I'm dead?

By day we irritate each other, unwitting.
At breakfast, say, over burned toast.

By night, over the black potholes
of the snores between us I reach out

for you and find only
a piece of bare, unfeeling

forearm. This flesh

7

I touch so carefully in the dark
ignores me, in its sleep

indifferent, cold, unknowing
as the cold hiss of the ocean

and who we are is buried in it.

I know you'd mother me
forever, and I you,

but here, at the end of everything
we know

as waves spill themselves on the beach
in foaming avalanches, crackling

stone suckles stone. Even the kindest

words scrape against each other like seashells;
flesh, kneecaps, numb lips

nearly raw now, almost ready to break up,

crumble themselves into that loud
nameless energy we must return to

and can't, not yet,
nervously tying our pajamas

as tight as we can against the taut
temporary skin

of the bodies we tremble across the world in.

What Love Does
(with Tear-Floods and Sigh-Tempests)

Fused together. After years
            and years of it, mostly the two legs
    of the one couple move easily,
               the rickety stick figure teeters
  on its tall stilts giraffe-like, gracefully gangling
      almost without thinking about it, but sometimes

Out of nowhere, at cross-eyed
      "dull sublunary" purposes or just
            for no reason, suddenly
  the opposite legs begin walking
      straight into it, *Ambush*
  first one yells

Then the other, black expletives staccato,
    explode across the room like bullets, Oh, oh,
      it's your fault,
    all *I* did was, I can't

Stand it, hoarsely the one shouts, red-faced,
    then the other's knees
        crumple in the blast, screaming
  straight fall to a floor bristling
        with fangs, hackles, flames

It always feels like, though there's nothing
         physical but emotional
    blows, bags of salt,

thieves' blackjacks pounding
                    over and over, sock, sock
          on the shoulders, on the head, but how,

----- ⨯⨯⨯ -----

This is all so tiny
          and so huge:
          holocaust, egg of the world
     smashed in one person's gut, listen
                    all I want is Justice, pure
          and simple, that's
                    right, isn't it? So

Now, trembles. Roars. Water
                    like toilets from red eyes. Wail. Wail.
          Where no one can see.
                    In the closet, the
          clotted stomach

Of the most private, personal
                    stone mansion or duplex
          crammed with nightmares, behind blinds in muffled
                    television sets muttering

Is where it happens,
          what, is this adult
          behavior or is it war is the only question
                    worth asking,
          here balancing on the brink

----- ⨯⨯⨯ -----

Disgusting! Because each of us knows
                finally not to betray,
                        kick the props out
                from under anyone, least of all hope's
                                double-jointed, stiff
                tall clown with legs
        and toes we know not to step on

But do anyway, all over each other's most
                        intimate territory, don't hurt me!
                Oh when
        did this first begin? Slow, seeping
                        how could we not notice it, the rot

In every faucet, urine green, suffocating
                        the whole household, yes
                of course we noticed them, the snide barbs,
        the lies, the sullen omissions

But never spoke of them, it's possible
                        some of us even wanted it, now, here,
                sharp! Definitive! The bomb
                        at the end of the world going off,
                the monster bear reared up
        on its hind legs with claws, with red slavering tongue
                        over the entire city, refrigerator in one paw,
                skyscraper in the other, with swollen
                                outraged cheeks stomps
                out the back door, good, good, O sweet

Riddance, parting is such
        delicious sorrow, at last
   finally I can give up, fall down in the shambles
          I really am, as misery sweeps us away

Helpless, I swear it,
        blameless before that animal
   I live beside, hating
         what I used to love, Oh
but it's so terrifying to be two, first one

Then the other weeps, shivers, then both run
      back into their own forested
          kitchens, bedrooms, caged
 circus lions that cower, snarling

And furiously whimpering, black golfballs
        run down the face as the house
          quakes, jackhammers apart
   into two poles staring across chasms,

The bridge between them ruptures, heaves upward
        in great concrete slabs, jagged
    thoughts, wishes, legs broken
    like matchsticks!
      Sob, groan, snivel,

Behind closed doors they wallow but still need
                    someone to listen to them, just
          see how you made me suffer!
          Each wants to say,
       now you're through with me I'm nothing
   but a hole in the side of the house left
                    by a crashed airplane,
          chairs, tables, even the cradle crushed

Into blackened breadcrumbs but next, churning among the ashes,
               in charred emptiness dead-ended, first one of them,
          then the other starts to wonder
               is it possible the other's pain

                              —⊶⊷⊶—

Is as bad as mine? Out here in the cinders shivering,
               red-nosed, on one foot
          about to topple—oh
   let it not be too late, everyone needs two legs
                    at least, please, come back —

                              —⊶⊷⊶—

And slowly, heavily, the other one
               does!
     Literally, at the very door
                    of the getaway car heads
          homeward, over the collapsing bridge, with humble
               soft feet on the stairs, what's this

Gentle knocking, I'll pretend
               not to notice, why should I,
                            here huddled with my own wrinkled
        sour apples I tell you

Get Out Of Here but you won't,
                  give you an inch and it's Love Me
       Love My Camel, with sly
curly eyelashes sneaking through the clogged
       familiar keyhole,
                    with tender breath, with whispers

Stroking across deserts, smoothly
              over the bare bones of Justice,
            what's right
       chewed like an old shoe and useless but who cares,

—∽∾∽—

What happens now unfolds,
                 expands among the rubble
     as the squeezed bud unfurls,
               scraps of petaled red
     lips, eyelids, chests begin to breathe again

Beneath guard hairs bristled
              only to protect it,
       the hungry pet, the wild animal
   inside everyone, the raving
            irreducible I that finally wants —

See now—only the hushing hand, the heat of it,
              how like the thick fur
    of a coat in winter, the I'm Sorrys,
              the tame bear, the Please

Let Me bring you water, dry your eyes
                        by the one fire relax
              once more in the soft, soon-to-be-pulled-apart
          rough arms and straining legs of the other.

Light-Years

Under my hand mere

wooden, unspeaking
matter?

Your shoulder sleeps. But
to my senses charged.

The air around each
one of us is a shock

a flaming field or else
how do we know each other?

The body's log is a meadow

filled to the brim with
lost socks, or eyeglasses,

tiny, unseen flowers.

As you respond to a friend's
sadness, the tender

large box of your voice soars

everywhere, even as solar prominences
lash out at us with their long

fiery fingers,

their least traces, ancient
aftereffects girdle

each standing tree

only at the end to be toppled,
eaten into ash.

Light-years away, in the ice storm
the day my mother died

the lines were down

all over. No heat
in the whole town; we hid

under stiff blankets,
shivering. What possibly

could be left? Her favorite
willow tree had cracked,

lay there halved,
each limb sheathed

in its glassy shell glittering.

But shimmering out of the cold

frozen fall of its hair
that morning a queer

prismed radiance flickered,
flashed across the air.

Spinning before us in spiked
lavender, green, amber,

vague colors, elusive
small, diamond-faceted

strange sphere

it disappeared, naturally
as soon as we came near but

sometimes, just from the dazzle
of a pair of bifocals in the sun

whatever my mother was

or is, the
quick, sizzling power

of the body rustles

right here:

you, in your red workshirt
and jeans pulsing

sit next to me, in the rush
of violent, jittery

tenderness,

the sudden flare of feeling
we almost touch

Except for a Few Footprints

So. Yes. But still there is this peace between us
and under us, around us, over us.

Like spreading water, a glittering
feathery as white snow.

Smooth. Trackless. Sprinkled with
so many lights, so many sides to everything.

From the edges we look at each other,
about to enter it together.

Where does which of us begin
or the other end?

Blinded by so much white.

Outside the cabin
only the bristle of trees.

You brush your teeth by the sink

and I watch you: short, grizzled
peppery spruce of a man.

Once I thought we were opposite,
you with your eyes,

I with mine.

But now there is only this calm
white coverlet over us.

We lie here looking out

as if we were floating, the lungs of silence surround us.
Think of it, walking around

outside the window, motionless
from the same bed what we see

and never hurt each other.

With all our lives behind us
blanketed now, covered up

except for a few footprints, the heat of them
sinking into the snow—

so rabbits cross our paths,
and deer, gentle as princesses.

Then you turn over,
or an icicle falls from the roof.

Where has the world gone?
A truck rumbles down the highway.

Plumed veils sparkle:
faint puffs of breath

skitter away across the fields.

The snow around us is a quilt
of tiny, fierce eyes.

I kick it away, then pause:

tip up my head to the sky.
Out there in the cold, drowning

in deep space stars spin
like chipped ice, slowly around the poles.

I speak quietly of this thought. Small animals
come to drink at this same spring, don't they?

But you never left it.

You say my name, you remind me.
And I return.

Hardwired

It was late, late in the evening

— W.H. AUDEN

Zapped dandelions,
           blown streetlight heads — O hardwired
  vanity of the intellect,
        you, once so jaunty,
              maker and breaker of the year's most stylish,
    "whatever he put on looked good on him"
           approaches to God, higher-mathematics,
  Brooks Brothers shirts or casual
        (baseball cap turned backward)
cashmere sweater slung over football shoulders —

now look what you pick out to put on:
        old pants hanging around too long
    in an upstairs closet, loose
        hems slipping; so anxious,
  looking at me first to be sure
      it's okay, with spots you don't even notice
what difference does it make, you

whom I'd hurl myself onto the launching pad
        of a hissing and clacking satellite booster about to take off
      to rescue, bring you back safe and
    gleaming like Kasparov the day before he was defeated
      by Deep Blue, that coolly abstract
   vault of omnipotent
      titanium connections you helped program
yourself, we all did, but now,

chewed by the mice of age,
the random *cha-cha* of cells hacked
into smaller and smaller metaphysical tatters,

as snakeskins dishevel the bedroom,
under thin shreds of hair your head's
transparent as rice paper,
human eggshell crisscrossed
by cracked cellophane no self-respecting
intelligence, especially an artificial
chess machine, would ever admit to,

let alone any *broad-spectrum, synergistic*
multinational
faceless Corporation that supports it
against all the rest of us even as it stamps us
one and the same:

but whether the label comes from Taiwan
or Guatemala or Bridgeport
it never quite works;
for all the new clothes I buy you,
even the snazziest,

just take off your T-shirt
and there it is,
the obstinate, flawed, unrepeatable
sweet outline of the body
of the child you once were caught
naked in the bathroom,
from white chest to swollen
small feet still touchable, unique:

the smooth stalk of spirit
                    like the Prince you are because it's not
        Deep Blue defeats us but the deeper,
                    dumb hope that such massively regimented
                    mental Conglomerates
            can somehow escape the one, single
                    crack in the teacup,
        Time's famous chasm with the tiny bridge stretched over it

where you teeter, alone
                    in your Coca-Cola-and-mustard
            moth-eaten jacket tiptoeing
                    carefully across it,
                    still flashing your long-toothed
        speckled jokes like spotlights,
                    gold coins sprinkled across the sky,

with the flourish of an out-of-date silk foulard
                    or a yarmulke or a top hat bent
                    almost out of shape,
                    in your funniest clownsuit, your disguised
        littleman's warm body jigs into deepest blue
                    crackling space like the soft sputterings
        of heat lightning just before a storm.

From the Beginning

Up to the eyeballs. Choked in it. Our
                    selves, minds compleat
    of mud. Shapeless, are we?
                    Even as I sluice toothpaste, rinse,
what spins in the glass
                    every day is intangible
    vanishings.
                What we eat, *think:*
                            boiling water for rice.
                    And washing napkins, clear
    phlegm. Hair balls in the corner.
                            Outside
                berries, seeds in bear scat.
        Or pieces of metal, loose screws trampled
                            into sludge. Heavy garage floors whirled
            like glaciers around the world, giant
    glittering monocles winking
                    in the Eye that imagines All,
        massifs or
                    mites. Refractions of the most distant
                            galaxy but one,
            bigger, smaller than
                    EsMiss EsMoore at the railing
        bound outward, wandering
                        waterfalls of stars, stars.....
Motes on a glass. Sleek wriggles
                    on the vast slide smear of heaven.
        Arms, legs, *human beings,* oh
                        never to know you

again would be

   such waste,   wild, wild
the proximal cold mulch

   of rain forests, Peruvian
fire ants and faces,
the green globe cracked open

   like an overripe pumpkin, enormous
wet maggot heap

   of trashed statues,
what we do to ourselves, were done to
from the beginning, lost

   or gobbled up, for Whose appetite
invisible atoms, minced angels ground

   to pieces in the universal blender?

What the Dust Does

can't be measured. It filters everywhere, all night
in gray fluff over every book in the building;
I mean we're coughing up real dirt here, pieces of dried skin
from previous owners, the parchment of dead monks
and statisticians flattening out each pitched battle
in the graph of human behavior: the minute whiff of disease

muffles the so-called air vents with more allergies and smarter
viruses every day, odd incidents in the boardroom
bathrooms, in the baby-changing rooms, in the first-trimester rooms
for preemies the size of thumbs; in elder hostels the blank
white port-a-pots, the glazed eyes stare
from gaunt bones as mantles of mold grow
over the oxygen tanks; a shiver startles the hair on my arms
as clouds of pollen drift onto the windowsills

from far-off ponderosas, but of course, everything always impinges
on everything, in pale frazzled heaps
of lint and cat fur my study's full of it. Though this fuzzy veil
is only a temporary screen to divide, press its tiny grid on us
like nylons over the features of bank robbers and vice presidents,
Help! – I know I should sweep it but I can't,
not all of it, it keeps piling up

in almost invisible poufs of what looks like nothing
and isn't: in cereal-colored flecks
on the state-capitol dome, in muted gold
flakes furred over shiny fenders and wheels—aren't the wheels
and some of the dead limbs still moving? I can't speak for sand

on the riverbanks, crushed fossils, ground-up teeth from the bones
of old forests, ten thousand billion grains of it as many
as all the stars in the universe, those chunks
of infinite density grating against each other and sifting across
     my desktop

and yours too, I mean who are we really,
washing our precious faces, the film on the mirror,
the nameplate on the door, the impertinent thin grit
even on computer keyboards, what is it
separates us from each other? My monitor's dead eye
is an oasis rimmed with the skeletons of camels
and rusted orange machinery, data banks stuffed with corpses

that may not be disturbed, not even with a damp cloth,
certainly not with the vacuum cleaner's inhuman
demented roar: because in my study there are two sides
to every surface, even with old earwax, with dandruff,
with desert winds rising to choke us, in the dried-up depths
of every watering hole, who knows:
maybe there's still something hidden in there, something green
as it is invisible, flickering in the dust.

Lion

Not that grand, not that masklike
muzzle and stone eyes

yet.

But the nobility. And the
occasional roar.

Tossing his heavy,
proud head

as one bothered by
gnats.

So he ambles, on careful
small feet, unsteadily

through his days.

"Let him," as he used to say,
"not be nibbled to death

by ducks."

I say, who have
never known him.

In This Corner

For as we are hurtling,   sucked
                    down through the manhole
          out of nowhere
                    jetliner door blown open
          loud static deafening
                    hiss of air in the ears
                              lost voices   ragged
          all the years we have lived
next to each other talking and
                              talking

Suddenly you turn
                    on one foot toward me
          hold me and all terror
                    vanishes,
     in goose down and   of the flesh, purr
                    wordlessly mumble   absolved
          of all anxiety   muffled

In your arms catapulting
                    together down the steep hill
          of speeding time mindless,
                              two chunky bodies
                    swept up, out of the wind
          howling by but safe
                    fire soft,   embers
          thick cottony warmth
                              in this corner stopped
                    still

In the Plague Years

In the old cartoon the terrified
                   man and woman high up, each
          backed against the same building

on separate sides of it, tremble when all they need—
                   as on the suicide ledge the received
          wisdom jokes, *"Only wait!*
                   Around the corner there's someone
     you should meet" —

to find each other is to inch
          sidewise a few feet.

But you and I aren't
          done yet: as at our real
     live throats the hangman's umbilical
          barbed wire twists

till we start choking,
          almost at the last, self-absorbed
     gasp we crane our necks

one more time to see
     who's coming and then something—*what?* —

long ago hidden in our halved
          quivering egg-hearts shoves us

into each other's secrets as we grab
          quaking hands and jump

together:
        and now it's all falling
             as usual, but with you next to me

in such floating featherbeds
          of pleasure even on the subway
       going to work I'm smiling,
               grinning at myself in the black window.

Though we're only your average Jack
          and ordinary Jill now, with such tumultuous
       torn-up sweetnesses most of us keep right on
              kicking against each other,

but even with vicious love bites
        and tortured roars no matter:

in the wry comfort of jabber
          drowned in kisses, in fights picked
      for nothing and then forgotten,

do rainstorms remember their quarrels
        next day? Do avalanches
     apologize like adults?

The natural disasters of human
         intercourse are less elemental and more
      continental, even though they feel immense

as the mightiest tectonic plates grinding
          against each other and equally
     unstoppable,

all we really do is argue,
                    then clutch each other
            the harder, with this disreputable, angelic
                    love we go on living

even in the plague years
                    in Algiers, say, stubbornly heaving our boulders
        up the cliffs and down, poor cartoon
                    cherubs pretending we're not dying

anyway; on ratty slabs of cardboard, even on smooth
            hospital beds most of us do it without
                    even trying,

dropped over the edge
            like starved cats scratching
        so intimately in the bag

on the long way down, *get your hands out*
                            of each other's pockets,
        screech the wise shrinks as we plunge
                    faster and faster but still passionate

Collaborateurs? Sure, of the flesh
            only, but with such sweet
        however brief hugs, such hot
            however jumpy sex —

mired in it, the same soul doctors
                keep shrieking,
        mired in private matter and no one can rise
                above it!

34

But even as snow falls
          separately, each flake elegant,
     in lacy wings *dependent,*
               shaped by invisible valences and melting,

though there's no stopping them, the unknowable
          engines that started us, my closest
               and forever friend,

it's still here,
          this second to be held on to
     as long as we can:

though that it's hard to see, *blindfolded,*
          the shrinks tell us, by "projection," is it?
     —any more than the self

beyond the self is an agonized
                    rusty nail twisting
     in the hinges of my chest,

as distant birds move
          together and apart calling
     in the rushing night

now I hear you cough
          in the dark next to me the slight
     ahem I'd know out of hundreds and then you and I

together hitch up our courage and spit
                    in Death's and Mummy's
     and Big Daddy's one shrinking eye.

Old Hands

Months since we've made love.
No matter
I tell you, we're old hands

at this; so many
years I've loved the way you buttered
my toast, spread my strawberry jam.

I can wait. Only
once or twice I've felt
the soft grinding between my legs

flare up, beg to feel your
thick, juicy
syrups inside me.

Now, though we live on smoke
mostly, in the faint plume of banked
cookfires underneath my

thin blankets,
whether it's your hands
or mine fumbling

at the doorknob, it's your voice
in my root cellar always.
Sweet as canned plums

and other fruits, flashes
of fabulous jackpots
light up like furnaces, roast

goose in the pan, pâté
and fresh oysters, the dripping
horn of plenty flavors

everything we do, even the egg
sandwiches we eat stick to the ribs
like caviar:

because you make me
laugh, whispering bad puns
in my ear, curved around my

hips in bed, I'd recognize
your hand on my butt,
on the nape of my neck

anywhere. Even the bang of your fighting
shout, the shrill, rising
spite of mine back

excite me, shiver us both
like chips of wood in the up
and down drafts

of the blast of being alive
so long next to
each other: you have

only to breathe on me, brush
your palm across my cheek
and the oven starts up at once

with a whoosh, the flickering blue
secret geyser flowers
and flowers again, remembering

as far back as New Hampshire: caught
in the swirling smoke of the bar,
the hand you clapped on the shoulder

of the old bum and left it there
because he begged you, *the spreading
warmth of it feels so good, better than hot soup*

*ever was, please
don't move it* so you didn't,
all night long until the place closed

and he let you go, finally
to rush back to me, your black
Astrakhan hat sprinkled

with snow in the doorway
melting, your fingers blazing
at the latch.

Only Water

Every great civilization
we know by heart dries up.

Flaring across the heavens
who you are, that streak...

Spilled from a glass — the flash
soaks into the ground.

But that was in the afternoon.

On an overcast day how gently
you lit the scarred sidewalks

ahead of us and behind.

Fistfuls of running water.
But where are the cisterns to hold you?

Darkness beneath the eyelids.

You, whom I've never known,
I think you must be steam.

At the breakfast table, in the bristle
of pocket tornadoes you turn into whispers.

Lately there seems a transparency,
a barely perceptible wash

of thin, watery light
rippling across your face.

Out on the back porch
alone, staring across the alley

how quiet you are.

Because who else can we be
but ourselves?

As the stream roughens, as cooler air
coils in under steep banks,

waterfalls slide across rocks and then vanish
into dim gorges, changing

their bright bodies into spray.

As the moist breath rises
and then evaporates, buried

in underground pools, above them
rivers run like racehorses no one can catch,

here in the fading stain
of sunlight slowly drawing itself up,

draining away from the tips
of skyscrapers and bridges.

Certainly the Deer

Only a few places like this left:
low swamp, mushy, on the north side of a crisp
mountain lake. And you beside it, as if
you'd never used a computer. Or driven a car, or dined
in elegant French restaurants. Here, all's
clear, cold. Lush thicket, wet sneaker
catching muck—then, suddenly, the loud
quick ruffle of feathers. Where? What?
Loon, maybe, or pheasant, but no, *there.* Sleek
mahogany-and-gold duck sits on a submerged log
proud, eying you but also ignoring you:
this place may look safe, but Watch Out!

———— ∞ ————

toy schooner   poised
lost slipper on the brink

of Conrad's Africa, the massed
somber thick   continent

forbidding green   impenetrable
wall

pop   go the ship's
miniature cannon

three times   smoky
white spittle blooms

kids' firecrackers fizzle
and go out

on the Fourth of July   patriotic
cartoon balloons   swallowed

by Belgium, was it   or something
darker still   someone's

white boating cap lifts
three times   foolish

against the ramparts of night

———⊶⊷———

Meanwhile the duck begins grooming itself
calmly, with rude beak jabbing
its thick plumage, its deep brocaded coat,
over and over, the soft poufs of its feathers
drift across the water, in gauzy flotillas of fine
nested fluff like small pleasure boats skimming
every which way until there's an abrupt *whoosh*
on your right hand, in a startled corona of brown fur
a deer hurtles away from you, the wiry legs jackknife,
the black hooves kick backward and then out of dense
briery bushes, everything happens in a flash.

———⊶⊷———

But how is this possible? The sweet, high-flying
breath of Stern's violin

lands   so lightly, attacks that begin
with no force, the firm pressure deepening

only as the string consents, the colors of sunset's green
looping and then sliding

imperceptibly toward brown, the catch in the heart's throat
rounding out into sorrow, not colonized

but *lived,* attended to, followed
like a whippoorwill's cry, the meaning almost caught

but then not; suddenly the sound springs
into new woods,   *who made this*

doesn't matter. Schubert once, but now everyone
wants to play; the fingers of the notes lift

like a fountain, higher and higher
after beauty we cannot have

but keep looking for, how else can we bear it,
the plucked gut rising and then falling,

endlessly reaching for the wild
agitations of air.....

As star-fisted leaves close like a green quilt
over the place where the deer was; trembling
the duck's still there, preening its iridescent vest
and keeping an eye on you but look, in the clearing behind you
it's the deer again, hip deep in the brushing surf
of silky swamp grass, casually lipping low willow
juicy mouthfuls, like someone moving languidly
around a living room, picking up a book here, a peach there,
once the deer even looks straight at you
for a long time, peering over its shoulder like the portrait
of a beautiful woman, the long, aristocratic nose,
the two dark pools of its eyes not even puzzled, simply gazing
peacefully, right through you, so that you feel—*what?*
Like a tree, maybe. Or a chair.

———✣———

Each fall we listen
to gruff voices   our children

muffled, polishing their
hot guns for the hunt

after them   the distant
beautiful ones they desire

to vanish into,   men
and women both   devoured

for days and days   on the trail
of soft, indifferent hooves

in bloody woods   struggling
not for music

only the minuets of swallows
after insects

at dusk   slapping themselves
they speak manfully

of timid shapes   retreating
even in sleep,   handling their

oiled rifles,   such insignificant
tiny machines drumming

against the wild wall
of the Rockies

thrust up,   panting
to kill what they need

to become

Back at camp, with the tents huddling
smaller and smaller, the raw, jagged
white teeth of the mountains scrape the stars
high overhead, at twilight they loom down on you
hunkered there like a rowboat, a crumpled shoe abandoned
on the edge of the lake; as water fills up the footprints you made
only this afternoon, that one moment you stood there

in the underbrush, words stick in your throat
like leaves, like burrs in your thick hair
in the middle of the narrow twisting path trampled
by various small animals: yourself, rabbits, skunks,
maybe even the duck waddling, certainly the deer
now clearly visible, now disappearing slowly into the swamp.

Lacrimae Rerum

Dogs yap, sirens wail through the city.
                              Air raid, ambulance:
lone bobby pin like an insect crushed in a corner.
              And teacups, abandoned hubcaps.
       Or beer bottles, and the cracked lips that swigged them,
                        or the quick blurt
and stutter of soldiers' feet.
                   But the lovers pay no attention, when does anyone listen
       to chairs, to the kitchen table with its mute
                     self-effacing surfaces?
         The backseats of cars sag
       beneath toys, cigarette butts, plastic
                          Dairy Queen cups, and chewing gum.
     The egg timer sits on its shelf, a sneaker
                curls inconsolably in the closet,
and then there's the doorknob, that once turned
                              easily in the hand, the cruel
              entrances and the exits, the keys
                frozen now,
                          motionless in a foreign pocket
because metal has its own fatigues;
                 stress cracks even steel girders, chipped plates
     and coffee cups touched by mouths
            that are closed now, sealed in the great silences
                of childhood:
as the lungs of the world strain
            in the bellows of a giant accordion of rocks, trees, rivers,
               and hollow mailboxes, all lovers inhale

only to exhale, like morning fog on a window
where night's breath weeps for a while
                    and then vanishes, finally even the sweetest
sexual damps and dews slide away.

The Brightest Light

Tranced, almost disappeared into the glare.

Like a dog in the sun he forgets himself,
barks dimly in his sleep.

Maybe it's all too much dazzle. Like the jellied
capsule around the eye of a cat,

Let's get out of here!

It seems to me he's a flashlight pointing the way
in pitch-darkness shouting

but maybe he's not;

maybe he's all chewed up inside,
minced into agitated neurons

pitted against dizzying shade.

Who knows what creatures may be skittering around in there
in the dusty garages of his head?

His hooves have always been small, clicking,
but his round voice is a barrel.

Confident as whales at rest, he was a fueling station

high over Colorado mothering
scores of pilots and satellites; I know

because I was there with him, basking
like a baby dolphin in his shade.

Well, he is the hero I made up for us.

Sunk in the dream of itself
the jaws of consciousness open, then close

at random.

Hold me, hold me, I cried out,
dry as a hydrant in a desert.

But now like flakes of ash

at the very beginning of a forest fire
something is starting to change:

Is it the way I see him
or the way he sees himself?

Always there are these vast, narrowing distances

behind our backs, stunt planes doing corkscrews,
black bugs in the brain sky.

Seasick, I think he must stop them,

but he just keeps sitting there
without moving; if there's a rope around his neck

he doesn't seem to notice it.

Meanwhile there are high winds in the trees
of all the nations.

Children are coming to grief,
cars burning in the streets.

In the brightest light of all,
I would like to catch him when he falls.

The Movie about the Dead Cellist

is perfectly straightforward: it's England so there's fog but also tea
and little cakes, the cellist and a bunch of his dead friends
are waving from the darkening front windows
of his wife's flat; she's still alive, they're pressed
close to the glass peering out, fluttering their handkerchiefs
and yearning over the young couple—his wife and his live rival!—
snuggled together, smooching right in front of them in the courtyard,
    but somehow
the friends seem to be looking at us also, in the last scene but one,

                   smiling, dabbing at our eyes with Kleenex,
what a good show we put on! And they appreciate it, like mild
vaguely familiar sheep, in their rumpled jackets
they're somber but not wistful; they're too full of themselves for that,
bat-faced, slightly astonished but also sleepy
like us, sometimes all they wish is that people would pay
just a little more attention to them, why doesn't anyone notice
all those holes opening up, inexplicable
gaps in the middle of sentences—

                still, even if it's only a movie
at least they're starring in it, looking out
so tenderly I can't believe it, probably it's nobody in particular
they care about but just life, warm blankets, garlic, hot chocolate
and hot bodies; in this bunch there's the cellist, a taxi driver
and maybe a seventeenth-century innkeeper,

                      their gaunt faces are sad
but not that sad, hanging around like slightly damp tea towels

in the home movies of our heads, they love how we keep watching them;
"Now *that's* gratifying," one says to the other, "it's nice to want and be
    wanted
whatever the reason": they know most of us miss them
more out of fear than anything, afraid to be left by ourselves
or out there in the cold, past the red Exit sign, shivering
on glare ice, but here in the theater at least some of us feel better,

                    instead of the worst, why not,
we imagine the best; though the dead cellist
returns to his wife only for a few weeks, the focus
is always on romance because what else is there, though it never quite
    works out
the way we want it to: the husband must give up his wife
to the rival; though we try to resign ourselves, the living

            and the dead audiences keep sneaking looks at each other
over the heads of the lovers because it's kisses keep us alive, isn't it,
isn't it? But up there on the screen
those shady blokes are fading fast, as the credits roll by
we try to hold on to them, we tell ourselves we won't let the dead
    disappear
though it's they keep caressing us, we're sitting in their laps!

                Well not exactly, but the world's full of them;
sometimes a soft hand creeps into a pocket
because where else would they go, in the darkness at the end of the reel
in the twilit theater, the last images abstract themselves
into a chill vapor, the midnight migrations of birds
over everyone's heads, thousands of them, the Milky Way
crowded with stars, cars zipping by on the freeway

so fast how can anyone recognize anyone, because they left ahead of us
they're way out there by now, how could they let their bouquets fall
from the sides of the ship like that, as the ocean liner pulls out

                            from the gray dock, who's separating from whom
depends on where you're standing, dead people of the world,
Unite! Do we really love each other or are we just
terrified of the future, with no bodies but white handkerchiefs
in flimsy clouds circling, halos of seagulls wheeling
that never come to rest, out there dressed only in strips
of tattered celluloid swirling,

                            Stop! Nobody cries out,
we're too busy applauding, warming ourselves with the live feel
of our own hands, even as our friends' seats empty
all around us, even as we fly up
in our heavy jackets, with hats and scarves muffled,
over the departing heads of the audience fluttering
like ragged wings, like feathery balls of yarn
forever unraveling, forever trying to rewind what is unwound,
with fingerless wool gloves reaching for each other,
thin-shouldered, crowds of us clinging together
against the ceiling like bats:
invisible, making no audible sound.

The Key

And still the planets go by,
      the surface of the skin
                  around your lips rucks up like a disturbed lake
         where I keep knocking at it, *let me in, let me in,*
   as if you could answer but it's no use,
                neither of us has the key.

In so many sharps and
          flats,
     with so many sealed compartments inside us,
            all anyone can do is hover
        politely, out in the yard hurling questions
like pebbles against windows we can't open.

Once, nuzzled into your neck,
              for one second I thought I'd done it,
    climbed up to the roof and dived
        in there with you,
      but then you must have thought

another thought: next to you in bed
     I saw you swallow it, could feel it moving
          like a piece of dried apricot,
  leathery but still sticky around the secret
       gold pulp of the jokes you used to tell

just yesterday, when you were all succulent
      limber muscle,
   when the tough little

skiff of your body used to bob generously
from one cluster to another at cocktail parties, my one

friend in the rain, astronaut
of lost souls, with a single insight
it seemed you could erase light-years,
bridge the unbridgeable
distances between us but of course

you couldn't,
even with NASA's best instruments for analyzing
each piece of subsoil for the precise moisture
and mineral contents of each casual remark
from strange worlds none of us can ever know...

And yet you're still here
beside me, in the deep husk of the bed
tucked against my hips
like the other half of an egg, bearded
teakettle of the blood bubbling

with such heat, beneath the touch of my hand,
deep in the burning shores
of what's inside you, with so many
streams of images gurgling, faint
fragments darting and whirling

I can't stop listening, quietly
all night to the bump
and whisper of your dreams.
With the waters of you muttering
like the hollow chunk of waves lapping against boats
in a boathouse, O ghost

Man in the Moon,
                    the absence of any one of us is visible

in all the houses on Earth,
                              even when they're grass huts
              in Africa, on the other side of the
                    globe from you and me,
                                   in each of us there's the same
       fluid slosh, impenetrable
                    pools of protein tangled in such familiar
              alien combinations,

moored next to each other we can only drift
                    next to brambled banks peering through dark windows,
              next to graveled jaws or smooth,
                              separate in space and limp

as wet seaweed, each in our body bags dangling
                         like soft jellyfish parachutes,
         shadows of white clouds sleeping,
                              layer on layer dissolving
              in the slow, blossoming traffic
         and wallow of seamless oceans.

Snow

Moon like an exhausted nickel.

Caught at the bottom of a giant
paperweight, cave of hysterical salt running

so fast nobody can hold on to it,
newscasters tell our fortunes.

Quick, come inside

says the man. *Come into the house
and be still,* says the woman.

As books nobody reads anymore vanish
into blizzards of fine print

Please, no more questions

says the president, throwing us his famous
curve snowball.

And then there are the trees:

what have they done to be wrapped in it,
caked, shrouded into white clubs

beaten almost to the ground?

In the icy air of the cave
the man and the woman crouch.

Breath breaks up into white noise
between them, nothing stands still.

The whole house shudders:
whistles around the chimney

or, someone's huge Hand

with a muffled thunk brushes avalanches
from the roof.

The woman says
Honey? one more time

as television circles the globe,
aerials strum the wind.

The Sea

Few think of its going on
when we are inland:

not whether the light in the meat locker goes off
when the door shuts, but the darkness
chewing away at the edges.

And now it's time for rain:

friends in the sinking ships of their cars
drive across their lives stopping for no one:

though we bang against the windshields,
make faces at each other at the crossroads

all night the sea hisses, rattles, booms,
in giant metallic thumps hurtles

into the vast labyrinth of an ear

where dying sailors shout against the wind,
in ragged silence mouthing vowels

we refuse to listen to: on the other side of the glass
landlocked, safe behind picket fences
and trailer parks, in the quilted farms of the Midwest

every once in a while, in dreams,
we see beyond ourselves

to the beaches of last summer,
seaweed oozing like brown blood,

magnets and powers long past but still present
in wrecked empires of timber
beating like fists against the shore

or caught, shackled, in cold caves rising,
tall spiring tongues
that fountain upward and then fall.

But these waves that muscle up the throat
are easy to swallow, the polite surfaces

of prairie sidewalks buckle
only occasionally, the sea has always contained itself
hasn't it?

From satellites high in space we see it
lapping at shorelines, with ruffled lace at the wrists
licking the frail bones of peninsulas

gently at first, but then heaving in its bed
heavier and heavier, stallion after a mare
maybe: as the thin walls shudder

great gallons lift and then comb themselves out
in long barrel rolls like the distant roar of traffic

on Main Street at midnight,

in a faint surf of words whispering,
dragged like driftwood to the crest,
then crushed, in a sea of fluent motion

that will not stop,
though it breaks off a leg of rock,

rubs several continents between its fingers, grates an entire island
into a heap of sand;

for all our glassed-in safety,
the ground we stand on is smaller:

men, women, nations in their salt howling
like hit-and-run drivers accelerate

over the twisting shoulders of water
that will swallow all of us, in the end

closeted among gaunt slabs,
blind carcasses wait like stiff overcoats

to fall inward, fall over us
nearer and nearer the doors banging shut
far beyond our farms.

The Things I May Not Say

Thirty years   now this
         what intelligences will you
      are you permitted to accept?
   At the borders of a new country
              I stand in the doorway watching
     your nearly motionless back.
   In pale cucumber-striped pajamas
           with the curve of your spine neutral,
     unemphatic as a comma

by day vigilant as a cat not to be stepped on,
        after hours of bitter contention
           because nothing's right
       anymore, words won't   stay in their places
   now, sprawled like a large child
          on my lap
    how embarrassed you'd be!

I would like to speak to you
        the way we used to,
      humming into each other's necks, close
    as tango dancers, step, glide
      embrace

before you were dropped behind bars
          I can't get through.
     But all I can do is stand here
       holding my breath,
         carefully measuring each

barely perceptible rise
                    and fall of your shadowy hip
          against the far wall.

In the stiff clutter of this room
          clumped on a chair your pants, socks, key ring
                         and pillboxes on the bureau stare at me
               over your rumpled shoulder but say nothing:

gnarled, patient, wrinkled
                         you are a scrub oak grown
          into an adult male
               with thick, secret
               turbulent inner leaves I can't reach
     without you.

The history of your life
          and then ours together,
               the velvet houses we lived in
     and the words we lived for, hunting them
                    with pen and computer, my
          twin hummingbird   flashing
     our bright mirrors at each other

is almost over now,   silent
                    the things I may not say to you
          pressed into giant slabs,
                         earth's strata thrust up
          against my ribs in heavy

jeweled layers, unforgettable

                    lapidary thoughts neither true

      nor untrue — all nothing,

              nothing

to what's buried in you.

With No Notice

For while we are eating ice cream
or scratching our backs, or smoking

it keeps happening,
the quietness of it, the lack

of any insistence, notice
even

just as we're clearing our throats
in the middle of the Mozart
Requiem, say,

the great chords stacking themselves

and then stopping,
turning the page, in the hush
of hundreds at once,

green plants silently bend over
and turn brown,

grass blades lie down, the water
just stops rising to their mouths

with no notice, someone   stops breathing

like a flower, while they are turning her over
to relieve the pressure,

but who knows where
the last puff

of soft air may drift

almost invisible   tiny
winged speck on the tip

of a jacket,
the collar of it, the Milky Way's

dust like jeweled seeds   who knows

how many millions of particles
in whorled thumbprints, snow

falling like salt on the tongue

in the drift of insects,
the near miss of comets,

snatches of music spin
into whirling fractions, motorcycles

suddenly familiar   roaring
along highways or halted

at strange Stop signs, in kitchens
blurted into odd silences

suppose there really is something
that remains

with toast coming up, a remark
quickly muffled

as near to us as it is   distant

the dry whisk of a leaf
on the windowpane

A Chunk of Mars

But the minute I think of any one of you I'm lost, all of you
rushing by me like cars, like race cars in a stream
I'll never catch, here stopped in my tracks

on a street corner in Times Square stunned,
standing inside myself listening to the hum,
the buzz of Being like an ant farm
on the fast track to Armageddon, a city that's breaking apart

every day into millions of tiny explosions. Though any cross section
of time's cyclorama is a swarm of heel-and-toe moments hurrying
like plastic sandals, like bicycles in Beijing,

all I want is to slip into your Adidas
as if they were mine, in the corridors of your cerebellum
listen to your doorbells, your boom boxes and beepers,
your string quartets and your teeth clicking, clap hands
for your wrestlers just as much as my tennis champions...

Or we could just hold hands. Snuggle.
Drink milkshakes together, you brushing
the flying grasshoppers of my feelings out of your hair,
I dabbling my hot feet in the swift rivers of you, I beg you

make me at home in you. If I could once
slither around backstage with you, in the middle of all those pulleys
what would I see? If I could look in the windows,

poke my nose through the velvety red folds
of your prefrontal cortices, would I be visiting

some entirely new civilization, the remote
green flashes of alien skateboards dashing about Jupiter, say,

or the temples of ancient Greece all mixed up
with the pork chops you're having for supper, such weird
smorgasbords we invent, the hidden wiring that runs us
is a lit console pulsing with unpredictable
power surges, continents of impulse whizzing

through such speed-of-light galaxies it's amazing
anyone recognizes anyone, which enzyme,
which chemical blip in the brain is doing what

to whom? The checkbook never balances,
the panicked sweat glands dissolve into roiling ponds
just to think of it, so many things done

and not done, there's hardly room to breathe,
no peaceful clearing where there's no motion
but the lazy fall of a leaf...

And even if we could do it,
escape, somehow, from the packed circuitry of self,
what would that change? How could I touch you, hold you

in whose arms? Because all we are
once we're released, free-floating, therefore without anything
even to bump into is trash, undefined
atoms spinning, bouncing off each other in the hallways,

in the living room looking for a chair to sit in,
for something to read besides mirrors, because I love you
really (*but what is that?*) I'd stretch like rubber to reach you

and probably snap; no more ecstatic lyre
or rock band or even flat disc burbling, but forget Orpheus,
no matter what happens, I'm still focusing
on you only, you peeling an orange
or punching a Macintosh, or standing at a window staring...

Even with all telephone lines down
in the eye of the hurricane I'll still be calling you
over the concrete canyons, the airports and the abandoned cow barns,

over the cruel dictators and the shiny brown globes
of tribal mothers-to-be, all those pyramidal
armed camps thrusting and grabbing, please

listen to me: because even at rush hour in the subway
there's more going on inside than there is outside;
in the shack, the igloo, the apartment building,
pressed in on ourselves, in all our intestinal cubbyholes

like overdetermined, headed-for-the-canning-factory
silvery schools of sardines, whoever you are I'll never
stop looking for you, in the limp braid straggling down the child's
        dirty rebozo,

in her brother's snarl, in the chili-pepper beads of sweat
on the gatekeeper's arms at the afternoon bullfight
hitching up his chaps, in the bum panhandling the alley

or the high-school Science teacher—what's she trying to explain now,
out of the piled-up cells boiling inside us
only to rise like steam, then condense

into broken guitar strings, crumpled pieces of paper
and lost earrings swept into every last corner
of Earth, with moles burrowing beneath us

among the microorganisms, the first swampy bits of life
left over from the beginning, even if we go as far backward
as we go forward, scattered among Red Dwarves
and tall space stations, sleepless eyes winking

over the jungle gyms of a universe
crowded with matter and curved in on itself, it's so infinitesimally
      empty
among the dots and the synapses I miss you, I miss you terribly
even when we're together, but one day
when a chunk of Mars drops into someone's cornfield I promise you
      I'll find you.

Moments the Body Rises

Heaped powder   hushed
grainy seas drift

between the trees   ponderosas

guardian soldiers thrust up
high on the peaks   silent

winds tearing at them   like teeth

cragged eyebrows bend
over white caked   chins

heavy with darkness
and snow

—⚬⚬⚬—

so we remember them, returning
next day to find them

glistening shapes   transformed
overnight into white

helmeted spires, the
pure, shining

history of change

repeated now in the skier's
tiniest concentration

the winter athlete's quick

jeweled springs   minute
hitches of ankle or wrist

———∞∞∞———

along the fall line pitched
perilously   descending

each encounter's edged
precisions to be met

fast, faster   these
shocks to be absorbed

by the whole body, the

arabesques of skiers

red, long-legged birds
like silk scarves   flowing

over white sheets

———∞∞∞———

pushed to the limits, such
leaps into transparent air's

blind arms, husky
heated forms twist

from side to side   thrust
in, out   alchemized

by their own speed   burning
liquid hips pump

———∞∞∞———

until it happens   suddenly

without willing it   effortless
moments the body rises

into cool fire   mind

and sweaty torso flame
among the trees   then out

to the entire sky

———∞∞∞———

up from their white crevasses
angels almost, with loose

arrowy feathered whips

in the vats of heaven swoop
against the blue   pale

twin contrails float
out of one wing   two

ghosts together   the great
spirited song of the legs

takes over, dazzling
white swords flash

as sinews stretch   reaching
out of their own heat

———— ∞ ————

into halos of ice, prismed
feathered flesh   skimming

each figure and its other
white phantom   moves

body to body pouring
molten, smooth as glass

soars upward until the whole
muscular sweet column

is a tree moving! Connected
between earth and sky

———— ∞∞∞ ————

in the faint, breathless   quiver
of sharp twigs   steepled

needles of white hoarfrost
crystallized sparks glitter

on the stiff branch
of a tree

diamond eyelashes wink
crusted molecules   dazzle

shaking their white hair
in the least wind   invisible

out of their own friction

smaller and smaller   microscopic
suspended fractions disappear

into the cold, blue
bonfires of air

From the Boat

What is it, then   between us
    in the press of parties   stammering
    in packed elevators   not meeting
        each other's eyes
       the metal boxes slide
    up and then down

as the sea roars   and turns over
        the land envelops us, out there
    rolling blankets   of trees
        the sky lifts itself
       into staggered blue
   distances

on the steel gray
      churning planks
          of the ocean
   gulls ride
      anxiously turning their heads

and crying to each other   mewing
       shrill needles pierce the air
     into shredded mist over oiled
           heaving green mountains

in the slick chop   in the long
     ponderous swells
    mates hidden   mothers

                    from their young

bob up   squawking
              teetering on top of one
                            wallowing wet sledge
        after another

who can see anything   from here
              a few small
                    damp fluffy dots
        on those vast   shifting plates
                    yammering

from the boat's exhilarating deck   rocking
        but confident   with binoculars
                    we look down on them
              and try to name them   who are they

all day we watch them
                    strange beings   feathered
        over each other's shoulders
                            surging onto the crests
              sliding into the troughs

Time Zones

Downstairs in Montana the phone rings and it's my sister
in Virginia, on the farm.

Five minutes from the hospital she tells me it's all settled,
they gave him the verdict yesterday and no, she's not crying,

she's packing her bags: in this speedy century
time turns even invalids into jet-setters,

six months into three cities he says he must see again,
has traveler's alarm, will travel, astonishingly

that's all he wants, from Washington to London to Beirut,
friends in each one and then on with it,

but first there are the odd jobs, the long grass to be cut
even in darkness, in summer shadows thronging

the headlights of his Ready Lawnmower flared
all last night, over the farm's lush front yard

furiously, not to leave anything undone
in the house with the new bookcases, the worn leather chair

she's sitting in now, telling me how much better he feels
she keeps insisting on it, while he's resting upstairs

she tells me they haven't been able to talk seriously about it yet,
back there in the East her voice clusters in on itself

in small, anxious loops, so what if she's a little high,
who wouldn't be, out here in the West taking the long view

it's the emptiness I can't stand, the prairie grass blowing,
miles and miles of it between one town and another,

fifteen or so states away it seems time can erase distance,
but it's the body must go everywhere and bear everything;

in a few hours they'll be off, jammed in next to each other
backward over the Atlantic, maybe then there'll be a chance,

with the moon and the stars hanging there, balanced on one side of
     the plane,
with the sun coming up on the other, red-eyed, waking up,

maybe then they'll be able to mutter something to each other
between breakfast and the hot towels, the stir and nervousness
     of landing,

but right now, in Virginia, the lab reports are all negative
for the moment, anyway, she tells me it's all right, don't worry,

I see her in my mind's eye trying to calm herself
the way she used to when we were children, with face muscles taut

as stiff boards trying to pretend she's okay,
she's telling me about some peony bush she just planted,

her voice snuggles up to it, anything to keep warm
while I sit here in Montana, in the cold,

holding my hand over the mouthpiece so she won't hear me
hours away from her and coming closer,

the trouble is we keep following after each other
and catching up too late: in the empty spaces between houses

the long shadows unfurl themselves
in the grass that never lies down, that wraps itself around the world.

Piece of Cork

But just look at him: "Bobs like a cork" on a stream.
Calm, minimally anxious. Passive as yarn
in his chair. Thinking about

"Nothing," says. Agreeably, agreeably

if erratic. Pops up like a pop-up
piece of cinnamon toast. With jokes,
flashes once in a while of

insight: "Hello, I'm back. Why do you look
so sad?"

Sudden openings in the tangle.

And the family steps on itself to answer,
"Well but, where have you
been?"

Do birds make
only nests of us? Against Earth's
mud walls, its mute

complicated comings and goings.

There are no chinks in consciousness
but what he tells us.

Stay, we beg him, *roar back at us*
once more in words

that will last.

The prairie wind sweeps over us with its incessant
final-exam questions,

but solid as butter in its sleek
animal skin, a cat can look out a window
all day.

Then he shifts in his chair
and we are all attention:

will he speak to us again

with the old warmth, the old
inflammatory light?

As heavy tree trunks nudge
finally toward shore,

stirring, he rubs his eyes. With the little sigh
of air going out of a tire.

But the hand's comfortable
in ours. And there he is, content
as a rowboat on a river.

Against the bitter carbon
of dried-up ink
"Relax," he says. With a twinkle

and a wink.

Not Ours

For locked in our separate pockets
of abrupt silence, clutching our hats and coats

as the lights in the cabin dim, the hulked body of the plane
lowers itself to the ground,

there's no stopping it, the final descent's begun
just as we knew it would, cinching our seat belts tighter

we can't stop yawning, stretched jaws creak open
and won't close, will they ever?

Already I think I can taste it, the dirt gathering in my mouth
in dark corners, at parties probing for buried cavities

I keep after it, but now, snapping our briefcases shut
and crowding into the aisle, it's so hard to let go of it,

the fist of fear, the tiny babyteeth gritted
that won't open, clutched in on ourselves

we're so anxious we *can't* speak, in midflight, chatting over free drinks:
what you say, what I say, what neither of us

dares to say out loud mumbles in our heads
like the low roar of engines, I want to say "Look Out,

you never know what's coming!" But can't,
we're so scattered it's difficult to think,

with gravity's huge hands reaching up for us
we can't help it, nervously holding on

to gloves, pocketbooks, keys:
after all, each of us has our own personal

belongings to protect; in a world disintegrating into loose
sketchy ideas, each explanation disappearing

before we can even understand it,
what's most important is the one thing

we don't mention: inside everyone whole traffic jams
of worried superjets circling round and round

like planets, crazy stacked-up stars sparking
and jittering, shouldn't we at least try to speak of them?

Because that's what it's all about; not one iota
of anyone's muffled sob in the bathroom

should ever be lost but it will be, so what if it's embarrassing
to open the door and find out we're all alike?

In the wavery purple neon of dusk coming down,
the shadows we cast ahead of us are heavy

as the plane settling, blurring slowly into endless
undifferentiated darkness

empty as ripped pockets, as yawns opening and closing, whatever
     happens
is not ours anyway, and none of us can hold on to it.

La Vache Qui Rit

Please, some Dignity! Sorrow, get back up on your throne
                at once, this is no time
         for Strauss waltzes. But perched on my rickety
             porch railing while I stuff marigolds in their pots,
         the radio refuses to stop playing.
               At the first awful oompah-pah
        my body starts swaying, in the backyard humming and jigging,
           bouncing its buttocks, flopping its shriveled udders —

outrageous! —while you're in the hospital, old friend,
           naked, far away in St. Louis
      with even your beard shaved, hooked up to all those cold
        Octopi tubes, robotic wheezers and suckers
             doing your breathing for you,
    the oxygen in my own veins lurches
              to a complete halt to think of it but excuse me,
        I've got to water my petunias —

And if you don't make it?
            The thought chokes itself off,
        then starts up again,
              Darkness rules the world
      in a series of bumps and grinds, a roller coaster
            of interchangeable sweats and freezes,
    as air creaks through the strings of your lungs like nails
        it's all any of us can do to stand it:

the body has its own agenda
            and follows it, yes, to the bottom

and yes, struggles right back up again;
                      as one disappears, another
immediately takes its place, it's disgusting,
                 poor butter-making bovine
but here's Strauss again, in the rich
             syrupy rollick of a Viennese love song
there's no help for it, with galumphing hips,
in draggled blue jeans laughing and then stopped short again,
          hearing your voice in my head
in case there's a call I keep the cordless
       tucked carefully in my shirt
but the radio still going, even though right now,
             stumbling from flower to flower and smiling,
there's a tear dropping from my nose and I must wipe it.

The Ground Beneath Us

For the end of the story sucks. Not air
exactly. Or gravel either. Nothing

to sleep next to. It reams us out like the exhaust
of retreating armies.

But you are a retreating army.

The roof trembles,
and the floor.

The shell around us is cracked

and you're in my arms, shaking. Over the crumbling
excavations beneath us. Where I won't,

I will not drop you.

Our neighbor walks in front of her tottering
mother, leading her on a string. *But not you,*

never you.

My old baby, my balding
word lover, all throb

and fire in my bed, such
razzmatazz!

And we were always equal.

As you took care of me
let me take care of you.

Dear lizard, dear snaketongue,
companion among the dictionaries,

though we thought we could write our way up
out of the battlefields of our lives,

look where we were going.

With your head in the clouds you mutter
We'll never make it, never...

But in and out of the overcast,

snow-covered peaks disappear
and reappear in seconds;

like the ghost eyes of portraits

the words you write precede
and follow us everywhere.

The ground beneath us is silent. But the dictionaries
and the libraries are still with us, towering

against the sky, Hellooooooooooooo
up there, yes you are the mountain,

the mountain the poem becomes.

Where There Were Once Trails

But what is it, the way the whole personality sometimes disappears
              like a field under a cloud,
                      like grass laid out flat,
      whipped by a giant hand into queer wandering paths, bald patches,
        clumps of ruffled hair?

If it's because you're ill,
          what is illness?
      Even though you're still in there, all systems presumably
             doing their thing, deep inside the dry
   closed mouth, the scowling compass of eyes
               irritably scanning the horizon,

where there were once smiles, wrinkles
       for me to follow,
             where there were once trails
    beside the creekbeds, what are these
       vague whorls of dust gusting across terrain
  I, who knew you well when you were well,
       have never seen before, are you well still?

Or perhaps we are all ill:
          like wooden flagpoles creaking,
      or trees from a train, or celluloid wheels turning backward
  in movies no one can see whole, continuously,
      you comb your hair, tell me you can't remember...

But usually when we fall
               no one hears us, let alone understands
            the little coughs and rustles
of bodies when they're alone. Electric branches,
                        bundles of nerves twitch
      like birds in the hedgerows, how is it,

you who are the turning
            earth to me, fresh
                 wildflowers wither on the table
     before I can reach you,
            the path home vanishes
     into the underbrush, tangled weeds

everywhere overgrown: each time I open the door
        whoever nods as I enter
              is a stranger;
   as the elderly rancher stumbles,
        as the sleepy householder stoops
          to pick up the day's newspaper, never
  from the same angle twice,

as dawn comes, that shape-shifter,
     rippling its sheets like veils over each shadowy feature,
            like swept grass, like trampled wheat rising,
   I keep looking for you but you're not there,
     whoever I thought you were has gone away.

Full Moon

We ran barefoot to see it,
         over the stony asphalt, surprise!
    Riding between clouds
             over the windy streetlight.

         And it —*she*— said?

Glacial. Naked as milk.
                Nor any galleon with swelling
                     smooth sails.

A woman's face?
        Turbaned, without makeup. Black
                     trees scratched her eyeballs.

             As if she could feel pain.

And we reached up to her,
             crying. Come back, we said.
    But she swam
        serenely on.

So I turned to you, beside me in the shadows.
        Don't be afraid, come
                 farther out so she can see you.

         But you hesitated, annoyed
                 at such foolishness.

Though she was pale as a wafer, perfect
                    impossible roundness soaring,
          you had so little time.....

                              ⸺∞⸺

Such an enigmatic
          blind stare:
          among the piecemeal galaxies the one
                              light that never winks.

Please, I said.
          Come down. And felt myself
    lifted up. Scoured.
                    And drenched, taking in

          gasps of rushing air but then left
                to my own devices.

With the hairs on my head bristling
          like tiny antennae, I kept listening for her,

        in the long sucking roar
                    of greasy kitchens, sinks gobbling and
          draining, I half thought

                I heard her but of course
                    not.

Because she is a mirror. Polished
          steel breastplate. Ruler of cities and books,

halos of timid self cast like a lamp
on the darkness above us but

we do not know it. O mighty
implacable Queen. With high
glittering cheekbones, swirled gray hieroglyphs
of man and woman both,

who can stand up to her? Complaining
contradictory Mother.

———∞∞∞———

So we are rubbed dull. Destroyed
as we are born again
over and over.

Because there are always fires
to be lit, medicines to be taken;

in winter boots or in summer
my feet are cold
every day like yours.

Hurry! You say
jingling the keys in your pocket
and I follow you
as I must.

With wild lymph cells, recirculating
rivers in our veins,

      we think we dream her up
    each month out of nightmare, O vast
      Empress of Helium—

but even as we turn away,
     dear hook, dear anchor
   and marrow of my bones

     there's no escaping it,
       inside us both is the sluice
   of her immense tides tugging us

     where we are all headed:

at the end of everything, in her massive lap,
      in palaces, cemeteries, *cesspools*
   always there is a falling
   off

—∞∞∞—

And then a rising.
   With the green fur of oranges,
     spores feeling around in darkness,

the entire soil of the universe
    turns beneath our feet.

On scrabbled peaks scratching the stars for sustenance
    but frozen, buried deep,
   scraps of fossilized life still thrust themselves up

96

in the jagged iceboxes of her breasts, O circular
                double figure,
        Lady most empty, and Lord

over soiled carpets writhing
                with colon cancer and mold,
        over duties with crooked knees
                that still have iron in them, over crusted dishes

with bread like boats in the oven, tall
                moonfaced ships come sailing:
        wearing her chilly cloak
                and his monocle,

        both of us follow her, proudly
                over the cliffs of midnight, over sheets of white ice

with whales sharpening their tusks
                and elephants, dead boneyards gleaming
        in the moonlight.

In the Long Run like Governments

Flattened,   in thin snow spread out
before us

the field cracks   like a book
of photographs   black on white

the two people walking
where it opens

up the spine   the path

on either side   slashed
stands of pine, deep

rust colored, red haired

rifles whistling
their black songs   the wind's

bayonets at the couple's backs

Someone should cry out to them Stop
Be careful where you step

but who listens   not chipmunks
screeching at them   from the trees

not eagles   imperial
murderers on their columns

of tall air   wavering

in the long run collapsing
like governments   who cares

who tracks up which field

the glass footprints
of deer like human beings

flung out over vast
wastes of snow like stars

wind   rakes through their fur
and our hair

the black letters of chickadees
like flickers of typescript   disappear

where the couple walks the valley
everywhere

saying to each other   What

Who speaks   bald
eagles vanishing

or trees

on either side   firs
once thick   now fallen

ranks broken, crumpled
armies lying in the snow

cigarettes spilled from a pack

no one can pick up
or put back

The Other

Out of the flux of light
        talk, coming and going
     naturally the one woman thinks
         she's just trying to comfort
   the other woman who is silent, grim
         striding next to her on the path
      beside the creek, through dappled
         brief woods
   in the shocked aftermath of death
         why should she bother to come back,
  take up the distant fingers
      of living again?

Chattering beside silly
      fresh creek water the comforter,
    knowing perfectly well how foolish
         maybe even impertinent
     it may be
  to keep going on as the other must,
      still nudges her
    gently, *When*
       will the kids be home?
because what else can she do, with the leaves already turning
  silently, into fall's
      raging decadence

But keep talking,
    never mind the submerged
      tense muscles knotted

behind the back, at the knee,
however painfully the blithe
ignorant current splashes
in and out of the shadows
of late afternoon bickering
right up to the moment
the other decides she has had

Enough!
Firmly her hand rises
rocklike, with no warning
plants itself on the first
between the shoulder blades, the warm
powerful deep shock of it
shuts her up, in mid–
urgent monologue cap–
sized, plunged to the bottom,
a writhing twig stunned
by the other's brusque
clumsy silencing but then

Almost at once she's back
helpless, bobbing on the surface, knowing
though she may pretend
she's just paralleling the creek's
mindless chitchat
for the other's sake, finally

It's more for herself, to forget
for a little while what's waiting
for both of them in the rapids
far upstream, where a blunt

underwater stone breaks
          the weightless white spray of light
      talk over its black
hidden back.

Where We Think We Live

In the silent house
he left her, the cat and I
visit, wanting out or
is it wanting in?

Everyone knows grief
can live anywhere. But it's
so hot in here. Hot and
humid. Wet leaves tap

tap against windows
he can no longer open.
Or drawers either, flesh
once solid as an oak

wardrobe filled with clean
shirts, ideas we leaned on, banged
our elbows against just
hours before Death

emptied him. Dispersed
each atom of him into
what's left? Dim, muffled shreds
of air still ringing

outside as it is
inside. Where we think we live
as if under glass, protected
as deep-sea divers

aren't. Tight-skinned, nearly
airless. Filled to the brim with
flickerings of hope held
only inside bodies

we can't leave, though we're
so mesmerized by the skitter
of shadowy live fish
out there in the dark

we can't help it, we're
so tempted by the hunger
to break out after him
we think we'd rather drown in

the attempt, burst through
all walls into bodiless
bits and pieces floating
everywhere, on both

sides of the window
jittering: here where we can't touch
ever, in grief's bell jar
neither each other

nor the rustling deeps
outside. For the same particles
that hold us in push us
apart; such terrible

pressures keep us alive
but stifling, peering out

at the wet woods, squeezed in
so tight there's almost

no breathing. Cat cries
to go out but neither of us dares
join her. In between gulps
of damp air we press

hard against the glass
between all of us but no
cat puts one paw over
the threshold and comes

back the same. Nor I
nor anyone. In these streaked
trembling tissues, in this
cold rain.

And Yet

there are so many islands,   sep-
                              arated
              in the brain.
        Walk across the channels.   Follow
                    a sandpiper

          Will any of us be there?

Clearer and clearer, at the edge
                    where land and sea meet
        everywhere, windblown
                        pebbles
                in all corners
                          and

I see you in the water
                    the veiled skin of it
          cloudy blooms of light
                        all who went away
              so many years ago   scattered
        dispersed   vaporized

              still here

I Dance with My Cat

I dance with my cat in the kitchen:
　　　　　　what idiocy in the morning! She puts one
　　　paw against my chin.
　　　　　　　Now, who
　　　　would grudge me. Not naked
but mistress of my house.

　　　　　As if over raked beds
　　of hot coals,
　　　　　　the tined forks of duty
　　and sadness-to-come bristle
in sparks from the closed drawer.

　　　　　　　Soon time
　　　　　　to turn on NPR, read the day's
　　newspaper, then you, the latest pain
　　　　　scraping across your face.

　　　　　　　In five minutes
　　　　I promise I'll wake you.
　　Meanwhile the cat purrs. Rumbles
　　　　　　in her throat. What handfuls
　　of innocent fur!
　　　　　With sharp claws sheathed,
snuggled into my breast.

Montana Pears

In the middle of Montana, eating.
What the man sliced for them, two pears on a plate
sprinkled with bottled lime juice
and sugar.

His fork. Then hers. Spearing up
naked, white-to-sour-green
chunks of moonless November's
cold orchards.

Tired, both of them.
On the thick, green
chemically textured part nylon
and wool sofa.

The man's comfortable
beige sweater bulges
next to the woman stuffed
into cheap stretch pants, a faded
apple red T-shirt.

Eighty years old.
And sixty. Add or
subtract a few. What have they been doing
all those years?

You, out there in the dark,
don't be afraid.
See, they're all lit up for you, do you
know them? I don't,

and I'm stage manager here. In fact,
I'm one of the actors.

A tape purrs in the background.
As the man forks up
the last piece of pear and puts it
in the woman's mouth,

Mark Daterman's electric guitar wheedles
over Glen Moore's acoustic bass in
"The Blimp Wars," two state-of-the-art
instruments plucking, twining around each other.

The next piece they play is named after William
Carlos Williams's "The Great Figure," in gold
reedy overtones, crackling halos of twanged
glowing noise, but then Daterman

and Moore stop playing, the man
says something, the woman nods,
thanks the man for the pears, I think he
thanks her for the music.

Pleased, both of them
peer at their books again.
But even the smartest, new
chemical preservatives can't help:

crushed, folded in on themselves
like sausages,
all the orchards are dark now, cold
shadowy fruit lumped
in heaps on the bare ground.

Silence. Then she stretches,
tucks her stockinged feet
in his lap. He strokes them
without looking, pauses
every once in a while to stare, rub his eyes
with the back of his hand. Well,

it's ten o'clock.
Soon they'll be going to bed.
Does the telephone ring? Doesn't anyone
recognize them? You, out there in the dark,
look in at the two of them,
glowing.

Alma de Casa

For last night, in your faded photograph album of a voice,
you sang us both to sleep.

Then I scratched your back for you
this morning, slowly, listening to your little grunts
of pleasure as we woke.

And just now, between us on the bed—rumpled ivory
no-iron sheets, cool breeze from the mountains —

there's a large butterfly, a monarch
with two immense wings, one heart.

As Earth Begins to End

I reach out my hand and it sinks through you
like soft fruit.

O tree to which I have attached my banner

I know you're leaving me
as you must; in the hospital you say my name

but I'm deaf, I can't hear you,

as the plane slides from the gate
which one of us is on it

and which left behind, I've never been able to tell
where we end and earth begins beyond us.

On raised pillows your face

like a book brought too close,
like the midnight sun blazing

out of all others looms before my eyes

until I can scan it no longer:
as loose cords slip along the tarmac,

I always knew this would happen,

but gluttonous for your body,
for your shoulder to lean on

and not fail, I plastered myself against you
like wet newspapers, like leaves

that think they will never fall:

even as all your arteries
and rivers emptied and filled, filled and emptied

I begged you to stay: O you
whom I have loved like oceans

though the harbor of your smile was generous

as the first wheatfields in Nebraska, clear
as the springs of the Mississippi used to be,

still I could not be stopped,

I kept on taking and taking,
I grabbed handfuls of you and ate them

and why not? Even in the bleak orchards
of hospitals, some summers end

only to begin again, fruit slumped into brown mush
revives, plumps itself into blossom...

But not forever. With these pages

about to be ripped apart among apples
that will never grow again, seas choked with oil,

with no furnace, not even an armchair to sit in,

the crust is thinner; even as I pull you close
in earth's threadbare jacket

slowly the harsh gorge rises,
tall column of salt growing inside me

like a skeleton, riven sword
of lamentation everyone must swallow

and can't; can't bind up the halves
of the split planet's blood orange

or button the body's last, unbuttonable coat.

Third Rail
(Autobiography of Lastness)

Because they are two old birds —
telling each other they are one.

       Because they are not,
       because they are more than one, and disintegrating

like a swarm of insects, brown midges over water
fizzing into the sun and then out, in the blink of an eye

      all brightness gone and nobody left but *us chickens:*

plucked, exhausted.
Left on the counter too long.

      Because we had to rest
      sometime, because —

              nothing.

     Scooped from each other's skin like cold potatoes

that got lost, that couldn't find their way home.

———————

See, there is this third rail running underneath us.
That won't go away, that wants to slice us into pieces.

In the middle of the most innocuous remark it leaps out at her —
No, it leaps out at him. Like a dog on a leash, snarling.

Down girl, down.

> Sharks on the prowl veer
> toward her feet, electricity swooshes through the dark.

"No, dear, the car keys aren't in the sugar bowl!"
she snaps: but couldn't this be funny?

> *Sarcasm, get out of my mouth.*

Because she thought she could carry both of them
all the way into the kitchen.

> Because she couldn't, because the high C of self-
> hatred spiders over cracked windshields —

And still she cracks it, the hissing whip of her guilt
all around him, *crack, crack* —

> Oh, she is shameless. Smart as a shoe with a pebble in it;
> here's gravel in her eye.

Every remark has its edge:

> Scratch others scratch yourself
> she knows.

She wants to forgive herself, can't:

> *O poisonous bee, tail that turns on itself*
> (in the blaming that is marriage).

As the rail slices by beneath them, the San Andreas Fault secretly
stirs in everyone's midriff

> *but mine especially,* she insists (all of us
> clutch at ourselves and insist) —

Because she only wanted to be one with him
forever. (See, it was never her fault.)

> Because there are two of them,
> after all. And no one's to blame, *no one,*

> that finally everyone forgets,
> that fire ants sizzle in their heads,
> that synapses break down and ooze

> acid neither of them can stomach:
> tangled nests of neurons, black

sparks spitting at each other along the crack

> *that was there from the beginning,*

in the cell as soon as it was born
forever fractured, even along the dividing

invisible line between the two halves
of the doubled cerebellum.......

———————————

Because it's all in their heads.

And then he erupts at her,
who else?

Shouts, hot lava boils over the stove

and out the front door: "I won't be back,
you'll see me when you see me" —

But inside her forever.

Yet she can barely hear him
over the burglar-alarm shrieking

that won't stop, that drills through the entire neighborhood
like a needle but what's missing?

Nothing's stolen that belonged
to either one of them.

Oh, maybe a few brain cells, a couple of old tapes
trashed. Scrambled. Discarded on the backseat.

But not by her, never! She swears at herself, Radio Signal:

Emergency. Program Over.

―――――――――――

What we gave up for each other, they think,

our own shores invaded until we are one
country with no borders, Help.

Because they are falling apart
together, falling apart

they keep picking at each other; stop, go,

as she makes lists for him, draws maps
which he objects to, or she does —

Anxiety churns the waters: red bacteria chewing
all up and down the Eastern seaboard.

So they retreat, almost back to the beginning,

they curl in their bed in the dark, grown couple murmuring
nonsense at each other, the sheer babble

and comfort of mindlessness together —

But sometimes the rail loops upward, climbing a hill.

Vein of viciousness, grim zipper whipping by —
which never moves, watch out!

Because we are one body.

Birthing itself. Into pieces.

The secret conductor of shock slithers through the water,

the jagged current slashes
between us but we are manacled together,

welded, then broken. Fused, but only until the final
infinite division:

the diaspora of stars

---

those cutouts of darkness, shattered pieces of light

reflections only: in scraps of paper, in snapshots,
in the brief minds of friends

arguing together, like streams in their beds muttering, in the low
backtalk of lives going by —

Because we are more than one, and disintegrating,

birthing ourselves into pieces.

Rage, rage, go away.
All the bright oranges are bleeding.

Oh but the one face

out of all others, the rolling voice like a bell buoy
still tugs at her guts, harbor she can't get out of

and doesn't want to:

because bodies live
by definition only:
                    inside their own borders and banging at them.

Outside there's nothing, *no thing*
but air the prickling skin shivers against

                    to protect what's underneath it:

the dim, private rasp
and gurgle of blood, the seven stopped orifices

                    choked, cliffed,
            like the sea beating against dry land

        even as they crumble together, *Hold my hand*

————————

she whispers, in the cry of seagull and rooster,
in the loud spittle of foam,

            — *"nor eye has seen, nor ear heard"* —

in the roar of the shadowy spirit breaking up

that won't go away without fighting,
on the edge

that was always there, dividing
and splitting away from itself, into infinity multiplying

as we who are one body

from the beginning seem to separate
into farther and farther waters,

as earth breaks itself up

into sorrow on all sides, into pain,
into meaner and meaner fractions,

cavities our sniping tongues
keep *picking at*

as if anyone could stop it, the jeweled snake
and piecemeal of stars chipping themselves away

high above us, in the light
that is all around us, under the crack in the door

at the bottom of the sea, in the fierce, unknowable
heave of wave and quantum

pulsing heavily upward, *Where are you*

she cries out and keeps on crying

as all that is inside *is dispersed,* shimmering
in the spume of a thousand eyes

       interminably flowing, in veiled phosphorescencies turning

   and turning on themselves, wave on wave........

Origins, Influences, Synchronicities

"What Love Does (with Tear-Floods and Sigh-Tempests)"
John Donne's "A Valediction: Forbidding Mourning"

"Hardwired"
Epigraph from W.H. Auden's "As I Walked Out One Evening"

"Deep Blue" was the name given to the computer that defeated the Russian Grandmaster Kasparov in a championship chess tournament in 1997.

"From the Beginning"
E.M. Forster's *A Passage to India*

"In the Plague Years"
A cartoon by Tom Cheney, from *The New Yorker*
Albert Camus's *The Plague*

"Certainly the Deer"
Joseph Conrad's *Heart of Darkness*

"Lacrimae Rerum"
Latin: "the tears of things"

"The Movie about the Dead Cellist"
Truly, Madly, Deeply (1991)

"La Vache Qui Rit"
The Laughing Cow: a French cheese

"The Ground Beneath Us"
Wallace Stevens's "The Poem That Took the Place of a Mountain"

"I Dance with My Cat"
William Carlos Williams's "Danse Russe"

"Montana Pears"
World-famous bassist Glen Moore and guitarist Mark Daterman make their homes in Portland, Oregon, and elsewhere.

"Alma de Casa"
Spanish: "soul of the house; housewife (or househusband)"

"Third Rail (Autobiography of Lastness)"
Wallace Stevens's "Peter Quince at the Clavier"

"Can anyone deny that we are haunted? What is it that crouches under the myths we have made? Always the physical presence of something split off....

Suppose the moment of Creation and our torn-off universe were recorded in the star-dust of our bodies?...

We are the beginning. We are before time.

... we compulsively act out the drama of our beginning, when what was whole, halved, and seeks again its wholeness.

Have pity on this small blue planet searching through time and space."
—Jeanette Winterson's *Gut Symmetries*

Acknowledgments

Grateful acknowledgment is made to the editors and publishers of the following periodicals in which poems in this collection were first published, some of them in slightly different versions and/or with different titles.

Beloit Poetry Journal, "The Dreams We Wake From," "The Ground Beneath Us"

Calapooya Collage, "Light-Years," "With No Notice"

The Colorado Review, "Snow"

The Gettysburg Review, "Lacrimae Rerum," "Where There Were Once Trails"

The Green Mountains Review, "From the Boat"

Gulf Coast, "What Holds Us Together"

Hubbub, "La Vache Qui Rit," "And Yet"

The Hudson Review, "Montana Pears"

The Kenyon Review, "The Other"

The Manhattan Review, "The Key"

The New Virginia Review, "Except for a Few Footprints"

Northern Lights, "Certainly the Deer"

The Pacific Review, "The Sea"

Prairie Schooner, "Not Ours"

Seneca Review, "Time Zones"

Solo, "Third Rail (Autobiography of Lastness)"

The Sow's Ear Poetry Review, "The Movie about the Dead Cellist"

Tar River Poetry, "Old Hands," "Moments the Body Rises"

The Texas Review, "In the Plague Years"

TriQuarterly Review, "In the Long Run like Governments"

Willow Springs, "Lion," *"Alma de Casa"*

Thanks also and always, for careful reading, for criticism, for nourishment and support far beyond the call of friendship, to Constance Poten, Debra Kang Dean, Patricia Grean, Deirdre McNamer, Alane Rollings, Sally Moore, and Kate Gadbow. And to Leonard Wallace Robinson, forever.

About the Author

Patricia Goedicke has published eleven earlier volumes of poetry, among the most recent of which are *Invisible Horses* and *The Tongues We Speak: New and Selected Poems,* named one of the best books of the year by *The New York Times Book Review.* She teaches Creative Writing at the University of Montana, and was married for thirty years to the late Leonard Wallace Robinson, a *New Yorker* writer, poet, and widely published author of short stories and novels.

Other Books by Patricia Goedicke

Between Oceans, Harcourt, Brace & World, Inc., 1968

For the Four Corners, Ithaca House, 1976

The Trail That Turns on Itself, Ithaca House, 1978

The Dog That Was Barking Yesterday, Lynx House Press, 1980

Crossing the Same River, University of Massachusetts Press, 1980

The King of Childhood, Confluence Press, 1984

The Wind of Our Going, Copper Canyon Press, 1985

Listen, Love, Barnwood Press, 1986

The Tongues We Speak: New and Selected Poems, Milkweed Editions, 1989

Paul Bunyan's Bearskin, Milkweed Editions, 1992

Invisible Horses, Milkweed Editions, 1996

The Chinese character for poetry (*shih*) combines "word" and "temple."
It also serves as raison d'être for Copper Canyon Press.

Founded in 1972, Copper Canyon publishes extraordinary work —
from Nobel laureates to emerging poets — and strives to maintain
the highest standards of design, manufacture, marketing, and distribu-
tion. Our commitment is nurtured and sustained by the community
of readers, writers, booksellers, librarians, teachers, students —
everyone who shares the conviction that poetry clarifies and deepens
social and spiritual awareness.

Great books depend on great presses. Publication of great poetry
is especially dependent on the informed appreciation and generous
patronage of readers. By becoming a Friend of Copper Canyon Press
you can secure the future — and the legacy — of one of the finest
independent publishers in America.

For information and catalogs:

COPPER CANYON PRESS
Post Office Box 271
Port Townsend, Washington 98368
360/385-4925
poetry@coppercanyonpress.org
www.coppercanyonpress.org

THIS BOOK IS SET IN MRS. EAVES, A FACE DESIGNED by Zuzana Licko in 1996. Mrs. Eaves is based on the Neoclassical faces of John Baskerville (1706–1775). While many type revivals leap into the digital age without regard to the technological disjunction, Licko sought to approximate the openness of hand-set type by giving the lowercase letters broad proportions. She named the face for Sarah Ruston Eaves, who was John Basker- ville's live-in housekeeper, and eventually, after the death of her first husband, his wife. Book design and composition by Valerie Brewster, Scribe Typography. Printed on archival-quality Glatfelter Author's Text (acid-free, 85% recycled, 10% post-consumer stock) at McNaughton & Gunn, Inc.